Book Sale   OCT 6

Oct 2017

D0392438

MANIFESTING FOR NON-GURUS

How to quickly and easily attract lasting results.

Robert MacPhee

www.manifestingfornongurus.com

Manifesting for Non-Gurus
By Robert MacPhee

Copyright © 2010 by Robert MacPhee

All rights reserved. No part of this book may be used or reproduced in any manner whatsoever without the written permission of the Publisher.

Published by HeartSet, Inc.
P.O. Box 232155
Encinitas, CA 92023

Printed in Korea

ISBN 978-0-615-32216-2

FIRST EDITION

"Increasing our awareness allows us to make better decisions and get more of the results we want."

— Robert MacPhee

With Appreciation...

We often take for granted the very things
that most deserve our gratitude.
— **Cynthia Ozick**

This book is a significant landmark of my life. It feels as though its contents have literally been gifted to me. The completion of this project would not be possible without the help of all of my family, friends, teachers, students and colleagues. It is impossible to mention everyone here who helped make this project a reality. And it is appropriate to mention a few...

This work emerged as I worked with the members of Jack Canfield's Platinum Inner Circle. I thank each and every one of you for supporting me as much or more than I supported you.

I am grateful to all of my fellow members of the Transformational Leadership Council who have generously supported this project. In particular, the mentorship of Jack and Inga Canfield, Stewart and Joan Emery, Hale Dwoskin, Marci Shimoff, Raymond Aaron, Pete Bissonette, Fred Johnson,

Steve D'Annunzio, Scott deMoulin, Dallyce Brisbin, Jeddah Mali, Lisa Nichols, Paul and Libby Scheele, Stephen and Alice Josephs, Robert and Cecily Scheinfeld, Jim Bunch, Alex Mandossian, Ivan Misner, Martin Rutte, Lynne Twist, Sydney Cresci and James Redmond has been invaluable. And I am especially grateful to Mike Foster without whose invitation I might never have been a part of this amazing group.

I appreciate my Mastermind partners Teresa Huggins, Deb Sandella, Lila Larson, Peggy Cappy, Scott Schilling, Linda Ruby, Stephanie Perez and Mark Haynes who have supported me and held me accountable along the way.

I appreciate all of those who I have served with on the world's most amazing event assisting teams. Thank you for showing me in real terms that it is possible to quickly and easily attract magnificent results. I am especially grateful to Jesse Ianniello for proving that "it does not need to be difficult".

I am grateful to all of those who enrolled in our first Manifesting teleseminars and our live event in May of 2009. I will forever be grateful for the faith you showed and the insights you shared. This book would not have been the same without your contribution. To Mike D'Alessio, Liz Buchanan,

Sherry McCool and Kim Mylls I especially thank you for stretching me to play a bigger game.

To Beth Weiler for being willing to take on task after task despite the fact that each one was new and required a learning curve. You allowed me to learn at a deep level that I do not need to do it all myself.

And finally to my family who have been so supportive and without whom this book would not have been possible and would be without meaning. To my parents Nancy and Chet MacPhee who have always been 100% supportive of my work, my in-laws John and Brenda Blom who have always treated me as they would their own son, to my three amazing children Kellie, Duncan and Lise who demonstrate for me every day how important this work really is and to my wife Pam who has shown levels of patience and support beyond human comprehension as this journey has unfolded.

Contents

"You are the way you are because that's the way you want to be. If you really wanted to be any different, you would be in the process of changing right now."

— Fred Smith: Founder, Federal Express

Introduction

Manifesting for Non Gurus is a profoundly simple approach to everyday life which is intended to help you quickly and easily attract lasting results. The approach is designed to accelerate the results you get when you decide it is time for a change.

"Manifesting"…it sounds magical, doesn't it? Almost too good to be true. But the fact is, it is possible to attract the results you want quickly and easily. Think about it; you have certainly manifested before. Just the right person showed up to help you at just the right time, the money to pay a bill that was due showed up from an unexpected source just when you needed it, you were thinking of someone, the phone rang, and sure enough, there they were. The question is, is it possible to intentionally attract results like this? And is it possible to do it more frequently and more effortlessly than you do now? The answer to both questions is yes, it is possible, and more and more evidence is showing up every day to prove it. Our clients, who use the approach you are about to learn, see faster and easier results every day. It has come to the point where every time a client calls and says "You won't believe what just happened!", I say to myself, "Well, actually, I probably will…"

If you are new to personal and professional development, you will find that learning the *Manifesting for Non-Gurus* approach is a great way to build a strong foundation of fundamentally sound information. From this foundation you will have a much easier time fully integrating what you continue to learn. The core content you will learn here is based on studies of what some people do that make it easy for them to live a healthy prosperous life filled with wonderful relationships. The approach is simple, practical and easy to use. You will also find that there is incredible depth in each of the five steps.

If you have already spent considerable time in and around the personal and professional development industry, I am particularly excited to invite you to try this approach. If you have read other personal development books, attended personal development seminars and listened to personal development audio programs, you will find that the simple structure of the *Manifesting for Non-Gurus* approach allows you to tap in to what you already know and apply it more easily than ever before.

The *Manifesting for Non-Gurus* approach is intended to be implemented with a journal, sample pages of which are included at the back of this book. (A hard bound journal to purchase and free downloadable journal pages are available at www.manifestingfornongurus.com). Your journal should be used as a way to practically apply the *Manifesting for Non-Gurus* approach. The information in this book has even more value when used with this tool for practical application. We use journaling as a daily discipline for several reasons.

First of all, journaling slows down the *Manifesting for Non-Gurus* step-by-step approach so that its impact sinks in on a deeper level. The process of writing forces the mind to slow down to wait for the hand to catch up. Second, the process of journaling gets your thoughts out of your head and on paper, establishing a baseline which you will be able to refer to later in order to see how far you have come. So often all we see is where we want to be, forgetting all the progress we have made.

I am a runner, and in races I often find myself doing what many of us do in our everyday life; I look *forward* and see all the people who are faster than me, the ones who will beat me to the finish line. I hear that critical "why aren't you running faster?" voice in my head. I only see how far behind I am and how much farther I have left to go.

I remember once, shortly after hearing that voice during a race, I looked back over my shoulder and was instantly reminded of how many people were behind me, and more importantly, how much I had already accomplished and how far I had already come. I immediately felt better. Although the second approach is slightly better than the first, both are based on comparison to others and therefore not ideal.

The fact is, I was where I was in that race. There is value in looking forward to see what direction I was headed and how far I had to go, and there is value in looking backward to see what I had accomplished already, but the fact is, I was where I was. It is the same with the journaling process you will learn here. Journaling each day, capturing where we are in that moment, keeps us focused on where we are now while reminding us of where we are headed and how far we have come.

Our specific approach to journaling is a powerful way to accelerate the process of establishing new habits and new ways of thinking. These new habits and new ways of thinking are what will lead you to quickly and easily achieving the new results you desire.

What we mean by "Manifesting":

Manifesting, as we refer to it here, is quickly and easily attracting lasting results from "nothing". By results we mean anything that we create and/or attract in the physical world. Cars, houses, relationships, the condition of our body and the emotions and feelings we experience are all examples of results. Any result we manifest starts as an idea, an insight, or an awareness. Where do these ideas, insights and awareness come from? Without delving into quantum physics, scientifically the evidence indicates that they come from "nothing", from a place beyond the physical world we experience with our five senses. Results may appear to show up magically, but here we will operate from the assumption that there is a specific pattern to how they arrive, and that as humans, we can have some degree of control over what outcomes we attract.

What we mean by "Non-Guru" (part 1):

All of us are manifesting every day. You do not need to live in a cave in India for 10 years and achieve total enlightenment in order to learn how to manifest. Information about how to tap into our power to manifest has previously been available to only a very small group of people. Now the pendulum has swung in the other direction. Not only do many more people have access to such information, but most of us have access to <u>too much</u> information as opposed to not enough. The challenge has become sorting it all out and finding what is most relevant to our particular circumstances.

What we mean by "Non-Guru" (part 2):

There are many wise people willing to share their knowledge and experience with us, and that is a good thing. However, we should not be doing anything simply because a "guru" tells us to. Our own intuition, common sense and inner guidance is more valuable than any external point of view.

I have (as of this writing) never been to India or lived in a cave, and I do not consider myself "enlightened", but I have been studying personal and professional development for the past 12 years, and I have had the chance to work with and learn from some of the most brilliant minds in the field. I have some valuable insights to share with you in this book, and I believe that if you USE what you learn here you will enjoy lasting results.

I do not, however, want you to do anything because I said you "should". My request is that you carefully consider what I share with you here and then decide for yourself what to try. Use what works and discard what doesn't.

What you decide to include in the way you lead your life should be determined by the results you get from what you try.

Most people, when they want to make a change, decide what they want and then almost immediately begin taking action. This approach requires a lot of hard work and effort and can, in many cases, cause struggle, pain and discontent. There is a much better way. The *Manifesting for Non-Gurus* approach includes setting goals and taking action, and it adds three very critical additional steps. These three steps are absolutely necessary if you want to accelerate your results while minimizing effort. Not including them is often what makes it so difficult to change and what makes results short lived.

At first glance, including the additional steps of the *Manifesting for Non-Gurus* method may seem to actually be more difficult and time consuming than "getting right to work". If you are thinking this, I ask you to consider an idea I learned from my dear friend and mentor Steve D'Annunzio, author of the wonderful book "The Prosperity Paradigm". Steve teaches a concept called "Hard-Easy", reminding us that when we take the easy approach at first, things tend to get harder later on. The opposite is also true. When we take the hard approach to begin with, and are willing to do the important work up front, things tend to get much easier for us later on. The small amount of time and effort required now to address all five steps of the simple *Manifesting for Non-Gurus* approach will certainly pay off for you in the long run.

The following chapters of this book explain each step of the *Manifesting for Non-Gurus* method in depth. At our web site, www.manifestingfornongurus.com, there is a one-hour audio overview of the approach which is available to you for free.

I'm guessing that you, like me, are a "Non-Guru", a normal person leading a normal life with normal challenges. Still, you are already manifesting every day. You are attracting lasting results quickly and easily. The question is, <u>what</u> results are you attracting? My hope is that the *Manifesting for Non-Gurus* approach will help you fully access and direct your manifesting power so that you can quickly and easily attract more of the results you truly want in your life.

This book and the accompanying journal are simple tools to remind you of what a powerful manifester you really are. Together they will allow you to learn and fully experience how easy it can be to direct that power.

Welcome to our community and happy manifesting!

Robert

Robert MacPhee

"Success is the ability to fulfill your desires with effortless ease"

– Deepak Chopra

Manifesting for Non-Gurus: A Five Step Approach

The *Manifesting for Non-Gurus* approach has emerged from years of observing people who quickly and easily attract lasting results. These are the people the rest of us look at and ask, "How did they do that?" and, "Why is this so easy for them?" The fact is, these people do a few simple things very differently from those of us who either do not achieve the results we want or have to struggle for everything we achieve. By making a few small changes, it is possible for you to dramatically change the results you get and the speed at which you get them.

An assumption of responsibility

Before we go any further, it is important to state an assumption. I believe that everyone who is attracted to this work understands, on some level, that they are 100% responsible for the results they achieve. By definition, the concept of manifesting is in alignment with this. YOU are the one who manifests your results, not anyone else, so there is no room for blaming, shaming or making excuses if you truly wish to quickly and easily attract lasting results.

My friend and mentor Jack Canfield teaches a simple formula that clearly explains the issue of responsibility:

$$E + R = O$$

This formula is the first of the 64 principles in Jack's best selling book, "The Success Principles". "E" stands for the events which we all experience in our lives; the circumstances that we are faced with every day. "R" stands for our response to these events, and "O" is the outcomes we get.

The important point is that we cannot change the "E's" in our lives. The world does what the world does. What we can control, however, are our responses to these events; this is our point of power. Our responses to the circumstances we are faced with ultimately determine our results. When we stop wishing the "E" would change and start focusing instead on our responses, we take control of our life.

MAKING CHANGES

Finally, before we get into the specifics of the five step *Manifesting for Non-Gurus* approach, we are going to take a look at a model that clearly illustrates what happens when we attempt to make changes in our lives. As was stated in the introduction, when most people decide they want to make a change they quickly set a goal and get immediately into action. These people recognize that their RESULTS come from their ACTIONS. This dynamic is illustrated below in Figure 1.

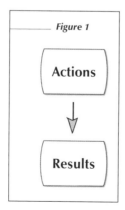

Figure 1

Actions

Results

The approach of focusing exclusively on actions and results requires hard work and effort. It demands enormous willpower and often does not yield lasting results. Here is why:

In order for us to discover a way to make lasting changes quickly and easily, it is important that we consider what precedes all of our actions. Figure 2 illustrates the fact that our THOUGHTS precede all our ACTIONS. Before we DO anything, there is a thought about it; even if just for a split second.

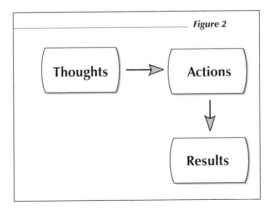

Figure 2

So, what precedes our thoughts? The most important factor in influencing our thoughts is our own beliefs, in particular our beliefs about who we are. For example, if I think of myself as a healthy person, I will think the thoughts of a healthy person, which in turn leads to me taking the actions of a healthy person and achieving the result of good health.

As illustrated in Figure 3, this pattern repeats itself over and over again every day in every area of our lives.

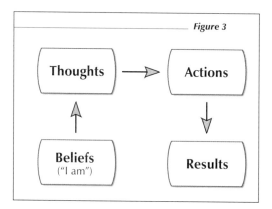

Figure 3

This simple four part model illustrates what is occurring both internally and externally as we go through our day-to-day lives being who we are, doing what we do and attracting the results we attract. The model clearly illustrates the meaning of two phrases you may have heard before:

Self-Fulfilling Prophecy: Starting in the lower left-hand corner of Figure 4, follow the arrows…When we have beliefs that we are a certain way, we tend to think thoughts that are in alignment with those beliefs, take actions that are directed by those thoughts, and get the corresponding results. Our beliefs about who we are literally determine the results we achieve.

Comfort Zone: When the results we get are in alignment with our beliefs about who we are, we are in what is called a "comfort zone". This is true even if our results are not what we want them to be or are not what we think we "should" be getting.

External Influences

Our beliefs about who we are are not the only factors that influence our thoughts. There are many other influences, including but not limited to friends, family, co-workers, television, radio, newspapers, magazines, books, and the internet. For the purpose of this model we will lump all of these factors into a category called "External Influences". It is crucial to be grounded in a very powerful "I am" belief so that these external influences do not end up determining our thoughts, actions and results.

Typically, when we state our belief about who we are, we hear a response. We hear that familiar voice inside our heads that either encourages us or, in many cases, argues against what we have said. In the context of this model, it is important to be aware of this dialogue between our BE-LIEFS about who we are and our THOUGHTS. This dialogue is our "self talk". If we allow ourselves to become too

Self-Fulfilling Prophecy

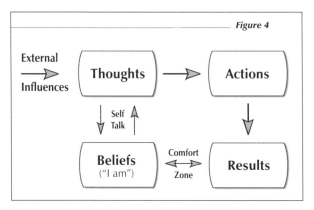

Figure 4

caught up in this self-talk, the danger is that we will never reach the action/results stage.

When the results we are trying to achieve are not what we want them to be, and/or when our results are not in alignment with what we think we "should" be getting, we often decide it is time to make a change. This is when this simple four part model becomes most valuable, because it clearly illustrates the reasons why most people struggle with making changes and getting lasting results. Let's consider another health example…

Have you ever known someone who joined a health club in January with a New Year's Resolution to lose weight? You know what usually happens to these people, right? Despite the fact that overweight people **know** they "should" exercise more and eat better, (external influences remind them of this constantly), the numbers are alarming when it comes to how many people join health clubs in January with the best of intentions and are nowhere to be seen by the first part of February. In the context of our model, how does this happen?

First of all, let's look at the initial RESULT: being overweight. Chances are that this person's current exercise and nutrition ACTIONS have created and are continuing to direct a path to this result. What happens in most cases to initiate a behavior change in this person is that an EXTERNAL INFLUENCE will cause him or her to THINK differently, ("I need to lose a few pounds"). The new thinking then gets them to start taking new ACTIONS, (i.e. joining the gym, exercising, eating better…), and these actions soon lead to new RESULTS…

But wait! What about that comfort zone we talked about? If the RESULT the person had started with was being overweight, what must the core "I am" BELIEF have been? Usually it is something along the lines of "I am an overweight, out of shape person who does not have time to exercise." So, when, in our example, the person starts to get new RESULTS from their new ACTIONS, they find themselves out of their comfort zone. Their RESULTS do not match their BELIEFS about who they are. So, in order to get back to their comfort zone they have two choices:

1. **Stop taking the actions that are creating the new results.**

2. **Change their beliefs about who they really are.**

Keeping in mind that most people make these kinds of choices unconsciously, which option do you think they most often pick? That's right: they stop taking the new actions, which brings the results back to where they were before and…ahhh, comfortable again. Or, at least, familiar, because as this example clearly shows, we are not always happy when our results match our beliefs about who we are, but we are "comfortable" as we have defined it here.

For most people, this cycle operates completely below their level of awareness. That is the power of learning the *Manifesting for Non-Gurus* approach. When we understand how behavior change works we are able to make better choices and therefore achieve better results.

Using the same example, is there a better way? Absolutely. The story starts out the same way: with a person having a THOUGHT that they would like to lose some weight. Rather than going straight into ACTION, though, this time they will take a step back into their BELIEFS about who they are. They remember that at their core they are a healthy, vibrant, energetic person - perhaps even an athlete at heart.

But wait, here is another place where we can get tripped up. Last time we left our comfort zone when we achieved RESULTS that no longer matched our BELIEFS. Now we are changing our BELIEFS so that they will not match our current RESULTS. In doing so, we will experience the same kind of discomfort, a pull to return to the way things used to be. We will hear that voice in our head that says things like, "this kind of woo-woo visualization/affirmation stuff doesn't work!" But look what happens if we continue to affirm our new belief…

We begin to think the THOUGHTS of a healthy person, getting ideas and insights we were not getting before. This is followed by taking the ACTIONS of a healthy person, which eventually leads to the same kinds of RESULTS we saw in the previous example. We start losing the weight, we get stronger, we feel more energetic, active and alive. But this time there is a fundamental difference; this time, when the RESULTS of better health begin to emerge, they match our new BELIEFS about who we are. We have literally created a new comfort zone, and this is the key to lasting change.

<u>Important Note:</u> In order to create a new comfort zone as I have described, you will need to repeatedly remind yourself of your new belief, reminding yourself of who you really are in spite of what you may have previously convinced yourself or allowed others to convince you of. These reminders will stimulate new thoughts, and eventually lead to new actions and your new results.

The *Manifesting for Non-Gurus* approach that you are learning here and will apply with your journal starts with this concept of belief about who we are. This belief is the foundation of how we create changes in our lives.

With that in mind, let's take a look at the *Manifesting for Non-Gurus* approach one step at a time…

"At the center of your being you have the answer; you know who you are and you know what you want."

— Lao Tzu

STEP 1

Who Am I?

In the four part model we just outlined, we shared that the process of manifestation begins with a THOUGHT of wanting something to be different. In many cases that thought is stimulated by an external influence. In the first step of the *Manifesting for Non-Gurus* approach, we take a step back from that thought, allowing us to later make huge leaps forward. We will step back into clarifying our BELIEFS about who we are before we step forward into ACTION. This is just like an Olympic long-jumper starting way back from the jumping point and getting a running start before launching into the air. Just like the long-jumper goes "backward" first, we will go from our thoughts into our beliefs about who we are, ultimately allowing us to propel much further forward.

The first step in the *Manifesting for Non-Gurus* journaling process is to simply ask ourselves, **"Who am I?"** We will look at this question from four different points of view:

#1 - Your Core Self

The first perspective on "Who am I?" is to look at your core self, which is who you are on an energetic level. This is a level beyond your body, your mind, your accomplishments and the roles you play in your life. Of course you have a body, but isn't it true that you as a person are not just your body? Haven't you noticed that your body changes over time, but you still stay who you are? At your core you are what observes your body but not the body itself. Your body is like a car that YOU drive around in.

In the same way, you have a mind, but you are not your mind. Don't YOU observe your mind when you talk to yourself? Can you see how YOU are separate from your mind? Have you ever considered who that is talking to your mind?

You have thoughts, attitudes, beliefs, and memories but none of these mental constructs define who you really are. Answers, ideas and insights come <u>through</u> the mind, not <u>from</u> the mind…

> *"The mind is a wonderful servant*
> *but a terrible master."*
> **— Robin Sharma**

We have accomplishments like awards, cars, houses, clothes and other possessions, and sometimes we closely identify with these accomplishments, but at a core level we are clearly not our accomplishments. We could lose everything we have and we would still be who we are.

We all have skills and talents too. Things we are really good at and things we love to do. But these too change over time, so they cannot be who we truly are.

We all have the roles that we play; father, mother, brother, sister, friend, boss, employee, manager, doctor, lawyer, accountant, husband, wife, boyfriend, girlfriend… The list goes on and on. But again, despite the fact that we play these roles, they do not define us. The roles will change over time, but at our core we will remain who we really are. Our roles are, in fact, a way for us to express who we really are.

So, if we are not our body, our mind, our accomplishments, our skills and talents, or our roles, then who are we?

On some levels this is an impossible question to answer. It is beyond the scope of our language and our physical senses to fully grasp and describe. So, for the purpose of our journaling, we will simply do the best we can. We will remember that this process is a journey, not a destination. We will answer the questions to the best of our abilities and remain open to whatever insights emerge next.

Most people, when they ask the question, "Who am I?", going beyond their body, mind, accomplishments, skills, talents and roles, find that the response that shows up is a feeling or emotion. It is often the feeling or emotion that we most want to give and/or receive. From the clients we coach, we hear answers like love, joy, abundance, consciousness, and awareness.

"Who you are and stillness are one and the same."
— Eckhart Tolle

It is important to recognize that we are, on some level, the entire range of emotions. Every emotion has a way of showing up, sometimes voluntarily and sometimes involuntarily. There are some emotions that we like and some that we do not like. The *Manifesting for Non-Gurus* process of inquiry asks you to identify the emotions and feelings you most want to experience so that when you become aware of experiencing **other** emotions and feelings, you can intentionally shift away from them.

For most people, when we take a closer look at who we are at our core, we are reminded that we are much more than what we perceive with our five senses in this human experience. We have a soul, we are connected to a source which is much greater than what we see, feel, touch, smell and taste.

When asking the question, "Who am I at my core?", your answers are likely to evolve and change. In the beginning, as you use your journal, ask yourself the question and simply write down whatever comes to mind. Borrow one of our coaching clients suggestions from above if you'd like. What is most appropriate for you will eventually emerge as you continue to use your journal. Be comfortable with where you are now, and know that part of the power of the

Manifesting for Non-Gurus approach is that it allows you to more quickly and easily take the next step, whatever that is for you personally. There are truly no right or wrong answers here; it is up to you to discover who you are.

Napoleon Hill, the author of "Think and Grow Rich", recommends asking a simple question when someone else professes to know something they cannot know for certain, like who we really are or what will happen to us after we die. Hill suggests asking, "How do you know?" The question reminds us that sometimes we actually do not know. We cannot know for sure, but we can explore. Each of us comes up with the answer that we believe is as close as possible to the truth, the one that feels right to us. Although we may not be certain we are right, the exploration we undergo and the answer we land upon give us a very valuable perspective that most people do not have. This perspective will give us a sense of purpose beyond what most others will experience in their lifetimes.

#2 - Your Roles

Although we have already seen that at our core we are not the roles we play, our roles **are** one of the key ways we express who we are. As a part of the journaling process it is extremely valuable to consider what roles help us express who we are. Considering our roles and being aware of them will help us to manifest the results we desire.

If, for example, what you intend to manifest is better health, you may want to consider playing the role of an athlete. If your intention is in the area of career and finance, you would focus on your role as an employee or business owner. And if your intention is in the area of relationships, you would see yourself in the role of a friend, lover, spouse or parent.

The question of what roles we play is usually much easier to answer than the previous question about one's core self. Considering our roles as a part of the journaling process gives us a valuable context and clarity about how we will express our beliefs about who we are.

#3 - Skills, Talents and Abilities

The third way of looking at the question, "Who am I?" is to consider our skills, talents and abilities – what we are good at and what we love to do. Being good at something is our way of delivering value, and loving to do something is our way of experiencing satisfaction. Obviously, the ideal here would be to be in a situation where we are doing what we love to do AND doing what we are very good at.

I encourage you to take an especially close look at the activities you love to do. The fact is, as you do more of those things, you can get better at them. If, on the other hand, you are doing things that you are talented at but they fail to bring you joy, then it is rare that you will one day wake up and decide that you actually love what you are doing.

For many people, continuing to do what you are really good at while adding more of what you love to do is a useful approach. Doing what you are good at creates value and feeds the family! We need to be very careful about letting go of that. Moving too quickly into what we love to do but are still learning to excel at can weaken our foundation.

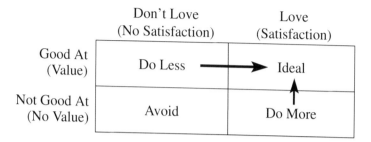

FINAL NOTE: Don't be fooled by loving being good at something! The appeal of this situation is probably based on other people's opinions: your love of getting the approval of others. This external motivation is rarely as powerful as the feeling you get from doing what you really love to do.

#4 - Your Contribution

The fourth way we approach asking who we are is to consider what contributions we want to make. With this question we look at the reasons why we are here and attempt to determine what gives our life a sense of purpose. In what ways would we like to see the world become a better place? The question we ask, (it is no coincidence that we ask this after we have looked at our roles, what we are really good at and what we really love to do), is "How can I help?" How can I be who I am and do what I love to do in a way that truly makes a difference? The answer to this question gives you a strong sense of who you are!

A note about FINANCIAL CONTRIBUTION: In this day and age, many people would like to manifest financial abundance. Many of us would like to have more money, but there is an important distinction about manifesting money:

It is impossible to manifest money.

What you *can* manifest are ways to deliver *value* and the resources necessary to help deliver that value. The money follows from the value.

Delivering value is one of the ways in which we contribute. If attracting more financial abundance into your life is an important goal, we suggest seeking out ways to contribute that deliver massive value. The more value you deliver the more financial rewards you can attract in return. Then you will be in a position to contribute financially, but you must already be in a secure financial position to be able to do so.

When it comes to contribution, money can flow to you when you deliver value or money can flow from you when you donate. Money is just a symbol. It is always associated with something else, a product, service or other exchange of value.

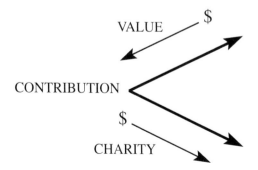

When asking ourselves what contribution we are here to make, it is valuable to look at situations from the points of view of others. Who do you want to help? How do you plan to help them? Instead of looking at what we want, we will look at what another person or group of people want.

Manifesting is not selfish...

Focusing on contribution reminds us that manifesting is not selfish. Some people believe manifesting is all about getting more of what we want even when it may be at the expense of others. However, when we make contributions a part of how we define who we are, we will find the exact opposite is true. We are all, at our core, generous, caring and considerate of others. When we act from that place, there is nothing selfish about manifesting at all. In fact, true manifesters, by our definition, are constantly making a significant difference in the world, improving circumstances for themselves and others.

Who I am is a choice.

As we look at each of the four points of view underlying the "Who am I?" question, a very important fact emerges: Who I am is a choice.

In our human experiences we get to choose who we are at the core level, what skills and talents we will use to express who we are, which roles we will play and what contributions we will make. Our awareness that we have this choice, combined with the ability to make it from an educated point of view, puts us in a very powerful position.

Returning to the four-part model described earlier, (the diagram has been reprinted below), we can see how important it is to be clear and grounded in who we truly are. Without such clarity we are left vulnerable to external influences. What we are seeking is a situation where the results we achieve are consistently driven by a clear sense of who we are.

Self-Fulfilling Prophecy

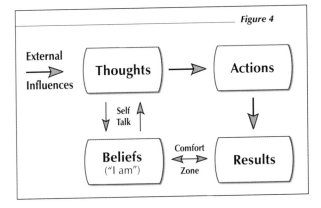

Figure 4

Great personal power comes from us having a strong sense of who we are. As this sense emerges, we will notice that we are less distracted from our goals and less easily intimidated by others.

The answer to the question "Who am I?" is unique to each individual. The *Manifesting for Non-Gurus* approach is NOT about everyone being the same. The process honors, respects and appreciates each person's individuality.

The overall answer to the question, "Who am I?" is a combination of all four of the points of view we have examined:

1. Core Self

2. Roles

3. Skills and Talents

4. Contributions

With a strong sense of clarity about all four of these points of view, we launch into the next step of the approach…

"Intention is desire without attachment"

— Deepak Chopra

STEP 2

What Am I Intending to Attract?

Because the *Manifesting for Non-Gurus* approach is focused on results, in many ways the second step could easily have been the start of the journaling process. In fact, this is usually the place where the manifestation process actually begins: with a desire for something to change. "Who am I?" comes first in our model because it is important to select an intention that is in alignment with our beliefs about who we are. With that being said, your success or failure with this approach will ultimately be measured by whether you achieve the results you had intended or something even better.

In this step of the *Manifesting for Non-Gurus* journaling approach we will ask ourselves, **"What am I intending to attract?"** This question is worded in a specific way. On purpose, we do not say "What am I intending to create?" because we do not actually need to "create" anything. This model is based on the assumption that the things we desire already exist in an abundant universe so our task is simply to attract them.

Not About What I Want

"What am I intending to attract?" is also a very different question than, "What do I want"? "What do I want?" is focused on lack, scarcity and need. Asking "What am I intending to attract?" is much more powerful because it is based on abundance, possibilities and choice. Ask yourself "What do I want?" and then "What am I intending to create"? Do you feel the difference between wanting and intending?

"I wants" can be very alluring and in some cases they can cause big problems for us, because they may be short term desires that are not in alignment with who we truly are.

Often the "I wants" are things we wish to *have* rather than ways we wish to *be*. In the area of health, for example, junk foods, soda, and candy are things we may want to have now that are not in alignment with the healthy person we hope to be. Advertisers are masters at persuading us to want what they are selling, regardless of whether it is in alignment with our best interests.

In the area of relationships, most of us have observed or experienced strong physical attractions, which are a powerful kind of wanting and often occur in situations where the circumstances do not align with what we truly want in a relationship. Being attracted physically to someone who is already married or in a serious relationship with someone else is the best example of this. Pursuing such an attraction can lead to indiscretions which do not take us in the direction of long term happiness.

In the area of career and business, a desire for money can get in the way of running the kind of businesses we want to run. Sometimes we are presented with a choice between short term profits, which we certainly want, and being socially and environmentally responsible or making a significant contribution to our community. The lure of short term profits can take us away from long term sustainable strategies.

The good news is that by using this manifesting approach we can often avoid this sense of having to choose between a "either/or" choice like profit now or contribution later and find ways to attract a "both-and" scenario where we do not have to compromise.

Recognizing that pursuing what we "want" can move us off track reminds of how important it is to have a clear understanding of who we are. This kind of clarity is the best way to avoid time spent on the kind of short-term "I wants" that take us away from what will be truly satisfying in the long run. One example of this is when young people are tempted with things like drugs, sex and gangs. Those who are clear about who they are as students, athletes and/or artists are far less likely to be drawn into these temptations. Drugs, sex and gangs simply don't match up with their perceptions of who they are.

In some cases, the things you want are irrelevant; like when you are negotiating a salary. You may have a certain amount in mind that you <u>want</u> to be paid, and your employer may have a certain amount in mind that he or she <u>wants</u> to pay you, but neither of these desires will ultimately determine your salary. It is the VALUE which you deliver that will make the difference. If you want to earn $250,000 per year but do not deliver enough value to the company to justify that kind of salary, you will not be paid the amount that you would like. If you do, deliver that kind of value, but your employer does not want to pay you that much, the value you deliver will allow you to get that salary somewhere else. Remember though, it has nothing to do with what you want.

Breakthrough Goals

When stating your intentions, we suggest that you approach it by setting a ***Breakthrough Goal***. A Breakthrough Goal, when accomplished, will open up new possibilities for you. It differs from another kind of goal which you may have heard of, called a BHAG (Big Hairy Audacious Goal

– a concept from the book "Built to Last" by James Collins), which by definition is a huge life changing, world impacting accomplishment. A Breakthrough Goal can be big, but does not necessarily need to be. The key element is that the accomplishment of it will open up new possibilities that are not currently available.

Small goals are okay, too. In fact, in many cases, smaller is better. The danger of too big a goal is that it can overwhelm you. You may end up spending too much time and attention trying to convince yourself that it's possible, losing valuable opportunities to get into action. Think of your goal as a golf swing. Consider how much further and straighter the average person will hit a golf ball with a nice easy swing, rather than trying to hit it as far and as hard as possible.

For the purposes of this journal, this second step of the *Manifesting for Non-Gurus* approach is simply a matter of answering the question **"What am I intending to attract?"**

As with goal statements, you should make your answer specific and measurable so that by the end of a certain time period you can easily reflect and measure whether you accomplished your intention or not.

Narrowing it down…

If you have previously worked on clarifying your goals, you probably already have a good sense about which area of your life you most want to manifest new results in and what those specific results are. If you are new to this kind of work, however, we suggest that you turn to *Appendix One*, at the back of this book, and brainstorm what results you would like to manifest in each of the seven areas of your life. Afterward, select one area that feels the most important and one desired result from that area to focus your journaling activity on. This one result will be your intention.

Keep in mind that it is perfectly okay to change your intended result in the future. There are no manifesting police who will be checking up on you. If you are not sure which intention to choose, starting by picking *something* is better than waiting for divine guidance and doing nothing in the meantime. Clarity about your choice will come quickly as you use your journal, and you will know in your heart exactly which result to focus on.

If you absolutely must choose several intentions, that is okay, but we recommend journaling on each one separately. You will most likely find that your sense of who you are remains the same for each journal entry and your separate intentions will emerge from that sense like the spokes on a wheel.

Here are a few examples of career/financial, relationship and health intentions:

- My book will be published…

- I will have five new ideal clients…

- I will find a beautiful, like minded and loving partner to be in relationship with…

- I will have open and honest communication with my daughter…

- I will reach my goal weight of…

- I will complete a half marathon…

Is your "Heart Set" on it?

Once you have selected your intentions, there are three key follow up questions you must ask yourself. DO NOT SKIP THESE QUESTIONS!! We see many people struggle to attract lasting results because they think they know what they want but in reality they are not exactly sure. Clarity about your answers to the following three questions is an important part of what makes manifesting so "easy".

Question One: Is it possible?

In order to initiate the manifestation process it is not essential to either know *how* a result will show up (you will learn more about this later) or to be *certain* it will. It is not even necessary to believe it is *likely* that your intention will become a reality. You simply need to know in your heart that it is *possible*. Just *possible*. You will undergo a physiological shift in your body when you fully grasp that your intention is possible. At that moment, the manifestation process becomes a game rather than a challenge or a problem. You then shift from focusing on the things that are missing or broken to embarking on a journey of discovery about how your intention (or potentially something better) will soon appear.

"Just hold the space that it is possible."
— **Michael Beckwith**

Question Two: Is it okay?

When considering an intention, especially when it involves a significant lifestyle change, many people become caught up in other people's opinions. "If I attract this result, what will 'they' think?" Not knowing for certain that it is okay to achieve the proposed result, they encounter resistance. Ideally, with this second question, we seek clarity that it is not only okay to achieve this result, but best for all concerned.

Remember, deep down, that what other people truly want for you is what brings you joy. They may not initially be supportive of your strategy because they think a different result will bring you joy, or they may be genuinely afraid that you will fail and therefore be concerned that you will get hurt, but in their hearts they honestly want what is best for you. If you have children, then you understand exactly what I mean.

Question Three: Are you ready?

The final clarifying question is also vital. While you are already manifesting every day, the *Manifesting for Non-Gurus* approach can dramatically accelerate the rate at which your results appear. Your intention could literally show up immediately. So the question is, are you ready to have your intended results NOW? Be honest. Does imagining having it NOW bring up anxiety or the feelings and emotions you want to be experiencing? If the answer is anxiety, it is okay to take it a bit slower, scaling your intention back to one that elicits the feelings you desire. All each person needs to do is find their next step and take it, however small or big that step may be.

Even after you have been using this approach for a long period of time, it is important to keep asking these three questions. Sometimes a "no" answer will surface after months of thinking the answer is "yes". That buried "no" could be just what is holding you back.

If you do get a "no", it may be something you can quickly and easily explain away. Bringing the belief into your conscious awareness is sometimes enough to take its power away. If not, it may be time to take another look at your intention.

Expect Turbulence

Lynn McTaggert's groundbreaking research in her book, "The Intention Experiment", shows repeatedly that it is perfectly normal and, in fact, to be expected that when we set an intention, circumstances can often get turbulent before they appear to be getting on track. For example, her organization conducted one experiment with a group of several thousand people who, over a period of four weeks, focused peaceful intentions on the war-torn country of Sri Lanka. The researchers were initially disappointed to see that violence in the region actually *increased* during the early stages of the experiment. Over time however, violence diminished and then retreated far below previous levels; in a matter of months, the war actually came to an end.

Nobody is ready to claim that this intention experiment ended the war, and it will take much more research to document the measurable effects of similar work. The more important point is that when you set an intention, you should stay focused and persistent, even if the going gets tough at the beginning. Initial turbulence appears to be the natural course of events.

So, now that you have set your intention, clarified that it is possible, that it is okay and that you are ready, there is one more important question to ask before moving on:

Is your intention in alignment with who you are? (If your intention is NOT in alignment with who you are, we suggest setting a different intention)

Assuming that it is, we are ready to move onto the next step in the *Manifesting for Non-Gurus* approach…

Recommended Books to Help You with Setting Your Intention:

"The Passion Test" – Chris and Janet Attwood
"The Power of Intention" – Wayne Dyer

"If it was the right thing to do, you would feel better right now. Do you feel better?"

— Casey to Jane in the movie "27 Dresses"

STEP 3

How Will I <u>FEEL</u>?

This is perhaps the simplest of the five steps in the *Manifesting for Non-Gurus* approach, but it is also arguably the most important. Without a deep connection to our feelings and emotions, we will never be able to fully tap into the potential to quickly and easily attract lasting results. Connecting deeply with desired feelings and emotions seems to be the main factor leading to the powerful "you won't believe what happened!" manifesting success stories we hear over and over again. If we do not tap into our feelings and emotions, the speed at which we achieve results slows to a relative crawl.

The way this question fits into our journaling process is simple. We just "flash forward", imagining that we have already achieved our intentions, and manifested our desired results. Then we ask, in that moment, "How do I feel?" Write down the words to describe it and, ideally, take a moment to close your eyes and fully experience the resulting feelings and emotions.

Feelings are the common language of manifesting, a language that communicates directly with God, the Universe, the Field, the Infinite Intelligence, or whatever you consider to be the source of all that is manifested. In your life imagine that there is a gatekeeper standing between yourself and the source of all that you desire. All of the communication you send through your words and your mind's images lands on her desk. Yes, in my case, this imaginary gatekeeper is a woman.

Her job is to avert unnecessary distractions from the CEO, who is the source of all that is manifested and has very important work to perform. I believe that as soon as I tap into the feelings and emotions associated with my desires, I can bypass the gatekeeper and send messages directly to the CEO. The deeper I connect with my emotions and feelings, the more powerful and focused the messages become. And the gatekeeper is not even aware that they exist!

"The Gatekeeper"

We hear about many people who set goals and regularly visualize and affirm what they want, but do not ever achieve their desired results. The value of goal setting and using visualizations and affirmations (affirmations are statements which create mental images of goals having already been achieved) lies in their ability to allow us to tap into the *feelings* we desire. Arielle Ford, the author of several books (including her most recent, "The Soul Mate Secret", about how to attract your dream relationship), uses a term we love. She suggests that we actually use "feelingizations" rather than visualizations.

> **"The real reason we do anything is because of how it will make us feel."**

Don't get me wrong here - I am not discounting the value of using goal-setting, affirmations and visualizations to help us get the results we want. The process we just concluded about how to identify what we are intending to create is actually a form of goal-setting. I believe that affirmations and visualizations are simple and powerful tools that create vivid images that connect us with the most powerful piece of the puzzle: the feelings and emotions which we expect to experience upon achieving our intended results. We must first take it to the level of feeling before we will accomplish the results we truly want!

Affirmations really are an excellent way to tap into our desired feelings. The words create an image in our mind and the image creates the associated feeling.

Here are the guidelines we recommend for quickly and easily creating powerful affirmations:

1. <u>Start with the words **"I am"**</u>. Beginning with "I am" forces the image we are creating to be in the present tense, and associates it with us personally. It ensures that we see the image through our own eyes rather than look at it from the point of view of an outsider.

2. <u>Be **Positive**.</u> Stating the affirmation in a positive way and avoiding words like "no", "not", "don't", "can't", or "won't" will create an image of what we do want instead of what we do not want.

3. <u>Keep it **Short.**</u> Being concise places the emphasis on what is most important and gives affirmations "punch". Also, short affirmations are easier to remember.

4. <u>Include an "**Action Word**".</u> Using an action word will take a still image and turn it into a motion picture. Movement makes an affirmation more vivid, real and memorable, making it easier for us to tap deeply into our desired feelings.

5. <u>Include a "**Feeling Word**".</u> You already know that this is *the most important criteria*. Including that "feeling" word is what will directly connect us with the powerful source of all that is manifested.

For some people, it is difficult to imagine the emotions associated with achieving a goal because what they intend to manifest is something they have never experienced before. It is completely new to them, so they have a hard time determining how the accomplishment will feel. If the answer that comes up when you ask, "How do I feel?" is, "I don't know!", then remind yourself that actually, you **do**.

This is a time when visualizations and affirmations are particularly valuable, because they allow us to "virtually" experience a goal as if it had already been achieved. Because our minds cannot tell the difference between an event that is real and one that is vividly imagined, if we visualize our achievement, we can then ask, "How do I FEEL?" and come up with a legitimate answer which matches our true emotions. Create the image in your mind and then keep asking yourself… "How do I feel?"

Many people spend too much time experiencing the emotions associated with what they do NOT want. Fear, doubt, anxiety and stress are all clear and powerful messages that are delivered quickly to the source of all that is manifested. These messages are a direct request for more of what we do not want! It is as if you want a salad, but instead ask for a sandwich, and then wonder why you keep getting sandwiches!

One way to elevate your experience of visualization to an even deeper level, is to create a physical experience of your goal being achieved. If your desire is to manifest a new car for example, you can actually go out and test drive the car you want to own. The physical experience anchors the feelings into your body, making them even more powerful.

If you are able to spend a couple of extra minutes on the journaling process, choose to linger on your connection to feelings. Imagine your goal already being achieved. In your journal, write down the feelings you believe you will experience in this situation, and then close your eyes and really connect with those feelings. Think of them as direct messages to the source of all that is manifested. This is true manifestation at work!

Earlier, we talked about how who we are is a choice. In the same way the feelings and emotions we experience are also a choice. This becomes obvious when we consider that the same facts can illicit very different feelings. My mentor, Jack Canfield, conducts an activity in his annual week-long seminar in which he has each participant explain his or her life story to a partner in two different styles. First, each participant tells the story as a tragedy, emphasizing the terrible aspects of the experience. Next, they tell the same story as what Jack calls "an upward-spiraling delight", focusing on all of the good aspects. Both stories are based on the same facts, but the feelings and emotions they elicit are completely different.

As you create your mental images and tap into the feelings associated with them, make sure they are FUN! Fun is one of the universal feelings we all seem to want.

The end result of the *Manifesting for Non-Gurus* approach is being actively engaged in the pursuit of our intentions. Our objective, however, is to be acting from a point of view which differs from that of most other people. The first difference between the two is being clear and grounded about who we really are, and the second is connecting to the feelings and emotions associated with accomplishing our intentions. Basically t*his means we are being who we are before we start doing what we do.* Again, this is a fundamentally different approach from the strategy most people follow, and it is the key to achieving results more quickly and easily than ever before.

Are the feelings you expect to feel when you have manifested your intention truly the feelings you want to experience? If they are not, then you should probably reconsider your intention. What is the point of manifesting a result that will not bring the feelings and emotions you desire? If you do undoubtedly want to experience those feelings, then you are ready to move on to the next step of our manifesting approach….

"It's not that we solve problems by thinking; we CREATE problems by thinking!"

— Eckhart Tolle

Letting Go of Attachments

Do you remember what we said earlier about how most people react when they decide that it is time for a change? First, they determine what it is they want (our step #2), and then they get right into action (our step #5). By using the *Manifesting for Non-Gurus* approach, we have so far gained clarity about who we are, set our specific intentions and connected to how we will feel when we have attracted our desired results. Do you see already how this is a very different experience from simply wanting and then acting?

Most people are also not aware of and/or have not been taught how to utilize our next step, which is letting go of attachments. Those who decide what they want and then immediately get into action are missing the sense of being grounded that comes from knowing who we are, the power that comes from being connected to our feelings and emotions, and the freedom that comes from letting go of our attachments. Just as having clarity on our intentions is what makes this approach "easy", letting go of our attachments is what makes manifestation happen quickly (sometimes even more quickly than you could have ever imagined).

<u>Detachment Is Not Apathy</u>

It is important to note that letting go of attachments is different from being apathetic. When people are apathetic they do not care about the outcome and are resistant to taking action. In letting go of our attachments however, we maintain focus on our intentions and are still ready to take necessary actions. We simply let go of the thinking that slows us down and gets in the way. Our objective is to act from a place of high intention and low attachment.

The mind is an amazingly powerful resource, but relative to all that we experience as humans, and to the infinite universe that we are an integral part of, the capacity of the mind is very limited. Much of the thinking which we allow ourselves to become attached to clogs up our "bandwidth" and prevents us from accessing and utilizing the intuition and ideas that are so important to this manifestation process. Ideas and intuition do not come from the mind, they travel through it. For most people, freeing the mind from its attachments opens them up to the awareness of possibilities which they have never noticed before.

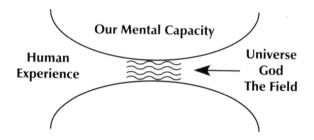

Tuning into new ideas and intuition can be like tuning into a radio station. When we are clear about our purpose and intention, we are tuned directly and perfectly into our "station". When we are off by just a little bit, though, (when our minds are dominated by unproductive thought patterns), we hear static. When we get further off, the static becomes louder. Noticing that static is a clear signal that it is time to "re-tune in" to who we are and what we are intending to attract.

Our thoughts are neither good nor bad, but they either support or do not support our intentions. In general, we are better off with too few thoughts than we are with too many. Again, our goal is to empty the mind of distractions and leave it available to receive the ideas and intuition which are critical to the manifestation process.

Just as we have done before, we will now look at letting go of attachments from several different angles. In order to complete this step, we must examine the things which we have become attached to. As we do this, we will again realize that we are speaking the language of feelings and emotions.

Appreciation

Generating deep appreciation for all that you already have in the area of your life where you would like to make changes is one powerful way to let go of attachments. The specific attachment we let go of here is the NEED to manifest whatever it is we desire to have. To achieve such detachment, simply consider and be consciously aware of all that you have already in the area of your life where you have set your intention. You can even expand this experience by reminding yourself of all of the things you are grateful for in every area of your life. When doing this, in many cases, you will experience a discernible physiological response in your body, a sense of letting go or opening up.

Next, realize that your life will continue to be wonderful (perfect in fact) regardless of whether you achieve your stated intention or not. This is the essence of detachment: being perfectly okay whether you achieve the goal or not.

Appreciation is very powerful! My friend Robert Scheinfeld, a fellow member of the Transformational Leadership Council and a truly brilliant mind in the world of personal development, was the first person to point out to me that money equals appreciation. Think about it…if you went out to dinner at a restaurant and had a fabulous meal and excellent service but there was no such thing as money, what would you do instead of leaving a tip? You would appreciate! Money is one way for us to show appreciation for the value that has been delivered by another. It is also a way for us to receive and enjoy the appreciation of others for the value which we ourselves deliver.

Appreciation is also magnetic; it literally attracts people to us. Think about it…aren't you attracted to the people who appreciate what you have to offer? And when you appreciate what others do, don't they also want to spend more time around you?

If a woman feels appreciated at work for the contributions she makes but receives no recognition at home for all her efforts, where will she be more inclined to spend more of her time? Relationships can literally be re-energized or healed simply by expressing more appreciation. Appreciation is a powerful tool for letting go of our attachments to "wishing things were different."

"If you can put your full attention and appreciation on what is here now, then you experience the bounty available in this moment."
— Lynne Twist, "The Soul of Money"

Expressing appreciation is a simple part of our journaling process. The other ways we will let go of our attachments do not fit quite so easily into the journaling approach. After expressing appreciation, we state our intentions and listen for what comes next. You know, that voice we mentioned before? The self-talk? That voice is often the best way to identify that to which we are attached. If the voice is supportive, congratulations! That is a good sign that you are detached. If the voice is not supportive, however, then it is time to perform what we call *"reverse or release",* taking those unsupportive thoughts and either letting go of them or turning them around. Here are a few examples of common thought patterns which we get attached to and possible ways to let them go…

Needing to Know How

The fact is, there are an infinite number of ways in which your intention could manifest itself. It is not necessary to know how it will happen, as there is no *one* way that it "should" occur. It is not necessary to do it all yourself and it is not necessary to be right. Although, it is important to know what step you will take next and it is useful to be open to whatever emerges after you take that next step, it is not necessary to understand the process that occurs in-between.

In the blockbuster movie, "The Secret", my mentor Jack Canfield talks about pursuing your goals like driving at nighttime. We know where we intend to go, and our headlights show us the next few hundred feet of our journey, but they do not allow us to see that final destination. And this is perfectly okay. After we travel those first few hundred feet, we will be able to see the next few hundred feet, and so on and so on until we eventually arrive at our destination…or somewhere even better, if we choose to change course along the way!

Needing it NOW

We see over and over again that the *Manifesting for Non-Gurus* approach speeds up the process of manifestation, sometimes quite dramatically. It is important to remember, though, that there is a gestation period for any manifestation. In fact, we cannot truly accelerate the process at all; it would be like trying to get a suntan really quickly…all that happens is we end up getting burned.

What letting go of attachments allows us to do is to stop *slowing down* the process. While setting specific timelines for intended results (how much will be achieved by when?) is a valuable way to create accountability and urgency, the best results seem to occur when we do not become too attached to our deadlines. After all, in most cases we are manifesting something completely new…how are we supposed to know exactly how long it will take? It may happen more quickly than we had thought it would, or it might take longer than we had expected.

The important lesson to remember here is that being attached to having something happen now is not helpful. Consider the attitude of a salesperson for example: Have you ever been in a situation where you dealt with a clerk who really needed that sale? Or maybe you have been that salesperson yourself. The experience is so different from one where the salesperson is instead focused on the value of what he or she is selling and is detached from whether he or she gets the sale or not. Which approach is more "attractive", making you want to buy?

A powerful question to ask yourself which will help with letting go of the attachment to *needing something to happen* is, "What is the worst thing that could happen?" That is, what will life be like if the thing which you want to occur does not actually happen? If you can reconcile with the answer to this question, then you have let go of your attachment to *needing it to happen.*

Judgment (Accepting and Allowing)

We also often become attached to opinions. Other people's opinions of us ("what will 'they' think?"), our opinions of other people (judgments), and our opinions of ourselves (self-judgments).

My Opinions of Myself (Self-Judgements)	**Others Opinions of Me (Imagination)**
My Opinions of Others (Judgments)	**Others Opinions of Others**

Others Opinions Of Me

How often have you heard someone say, "What will they think?" Many times, we stop ourselves from taking action and achieving results because we imagine that others will somehow not approve. We typically have an intense desire to be well-liked, and/or a fear of being disliked which can stop us in our tracks.

Let's go back through the *Manifesting for Non-Gurus* approach though. Would the people who are most important to you be supportive if they knew that you were pursuing a goal which was in alignment with who you really are, and would make a significant contribution to your community and would help you feel the way you truly wanted to feel? Of course they would be supportive and honestly, if you disagree, it might be time to rethink who you consider to be the most important people in your life.

> *"You are the average of the five people you spend the most time with"*
> **— Jim Rohn**

I am not suggesting that we should simply ignore what other people think. I actually believe it is very valuable to be AWARE of what others think, and of how our actions will impact others. This is called being considerate. I am only saying that we should not be DRIVEN by the opinions of others. If your intended result is in alignment with who you are, involves making a significant contribution, and will allow you to experience the feelings you most want to feel, then it would be unfortunate for the fear of what other people might think to paralyze you, especially since we do not know what they will actually think!

REMINDER: MANIFESTING IS NOT SELFISH!

When we consider taking actions and pursuing goals because of how they will make us feel, this approach can again begin to sound selfish. Remember the discussion we had about the difference between intended results and "I want"? We are not just talking about what would make us feel better in the moment. We are talking about aligning ourselves with our purpose and making a significant contribution, and that is NOT selfish.

My Opinion Of Others

The second type of judgment which we can easily become attached to is the judgment of others. It is natural to have opinions of other people, responding to the way someone else looks and/or acts, but we can get ourselves into trouble when we use a large portion of our attention and focus to hold on to these kinds of judgments. This problem often shows up as a need to be right.

My Opinion Of Myself

Perhaps the time when we are most judgmental is when it comes to our own opinions of ourselves. Do you remember the diagram we shared in the first section of this book, which explained self-fulfilling prophecies and comfort zones? (The diagram is reprinted on the next page). It shows that in the link between our beliefs about who we are and our thoughts there is an ongoing dialogue which we call self-talk.

Self-Fulfilling Prophecy

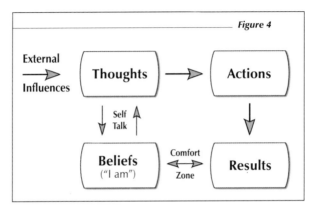

Figure 4

For many people, half of this dialogue is composed of a voice crying out for us to be all that we can be, while the other half is a critical, self-defeating voice which desperately tries to keep us in the comfort zone we described earlier.

In our live workshops we conduct a simple but powerful exercise to change the structure of this conversation. The exercise originally emerged when I was sitting in my office one day and caught myself listening to that same self-defeating voice in my mind. I decided, in that moment, that I was tired of hearing the criticism, and wanted to hear something different.

I pulled out a blank sheet of paper and began writing myself a letter using that same voice, but with one very important difference. I made the voice tell me what I wanted to hear instead of acting self-defeating. I told the voice to be supportive, encouraging, positive, and caring. I wrote two full pages because it felt so good. It felt as if the voice had wanted to speak this way all along, and all it had been waiting for was my permission.

In my case, an apology even emerged. The voice apologized for being so negative and promised to behave better. It was a profound experience, and the voice has been different ever since I wrote that letter. It is as if I gave that voice the permission to be supportive instead of self-defeating.

My self-talk voice still can be self-defeating, but the difference now is that I can more quickly turn it around. I still have the letter I wrote sitting on my desk, and I periodically read it to remind myself of how important it is to be kind and supportive toward me and my goals. After all, that voice is the one I hear more than any other!

SUGGESTED EXERCISE: Take out a blank sheet of paper and hand-write a letter to yourself. Write it using that voice which can periodically be negative, pessimistic and critical. Have the voice tell you what you want to hear, talking about things like what you have already accomplished, what you are capable of doing and what a great person you are. Just verbalize whatever comes up for you.

A simple way to let go of this kind of attachment is by remembering the following phrase: "Everyone is doing the very best they can with the awareness, skills, and knowledge which they have available to them in any given moment." Think about it; this is the truth. We are all doing the best we can. We may want to do better, but we will need more awareness, skills and/or knowledge in order to do so.

Here's an acronym to help you remember this important idea and to remind you that there is only one way to put yourself in a position to do better: get more **A**wareness, **S**kills and/or **K**nowledge. They only way to do that is to **ASK!**

Attachment to our opinions of others often shows up in our lives as a comparison. Comparison to others is a game which we cannot win (have you ever compared yourself with someone else and come out exactly even?), and it is a sure way to occupy our attention and focus with thoughts that do not serve us well.

Remember the example I shared with you about the time I was running a race and listening to my self-talk voice as it compared me to all of those who were way ahead of me? As I ran the race that was all that I could see: every person who was faster than I was. I criticized myself for not being a better runner, but then I looked back over my shoulder. I saw thousands of people who could have been looking at me in the same way! I was reminded of how far I had come and everything that I had already accomplished.

In reality, at that moment, I was doing the best that I could with my ASK. Some people were ahead of me and others were behind me. Comparing myself with either group was, for the most part, unhelpful. It would have been okay to aspire to be faster in the next race; I might have decided to set that as one of my intentions. And it was okay to recognize what I had already accomplished; there was value in that as well. Getting attached to comparing myself with others and using my focus and attention to establish one as "right" or "wrong", however, fails to support me in mani-festing the results I desire.

Letting go of attachment to our opinions of others and remembering that everyone is doing the very best they can with their ASK brings us to a powerful stage: **forgiveness**. When we truly forgive ourselves and others for perceived short-comings, we make a tremendous amount of our focus and attention available for far more important usage.

Guilt is another emotion that we can become attached to easily. It is another way we occasionally judge ourselves harshly. Guilt occurs when our behavior does not match our beliefs about what a "good person" would do. We convince ourselves that we should have handled a situation different-ly. We forget that we are always doing the very best we can with our ASK. In order to make the guilt disappear, we must match our behavior with our beliefs about how a "good per-son" should behave. So, we can either change our behav-iors or we can change our beliefs about what it means to be a good person.

For example: If a person feels guilty about eating too much ice cream, they must have the belief that "good people" do not eat much ice cream. In order to make this guilt go away, they can either change their behavior by eating less ice cream or they can change their beliefs by realizing that there are plenty of "good people" who still eat ice cream. Then, a person can decide how much ice cream to eat based on what is important to him or her, instead of relying on a random belief about what a "good person" would do.

Guilt occurs when we forget that we, just like everyone else, are simply doing the very best we can with our ASK.

Attachments show up in our thoughts as well. One of the most exciting aspects of working with people to make the *Manifesting for Non-Gurus* method a part of their lives has been that the approach brings about both an increased awareness of attachments, and creates a quick, easy strategy for eliminating them. When we become aware of our attachment to a thought pattern that is unhelpful, we can simply return to the first step of this approach.

Ask yourself, "Who am I?" It will be obvious from the answer that you are NOT what you are currently attached to. You are not fear, the lack of something, anxiety, stress, judgment or any other feeling which limits you. You are instead the feelings and emotions you decided you most want to give and receive.

When we let go of attachments, we free up our attention for other more important uses and clear the channels through which we receive ideas, insights and intuition. The time and attention we were previously spending on thoughts, feelings and emotions that do not match who we are and do not support us in getting where we want to go, are now freed up. When our minds are filled with idle chatter, judgment, worry and fear, we cannot hear the most valuable ideas, insights and intuitive messages. This is the power associated with letting go of attachments.

It is possible to more easily release an emotion AND decrease the likelihood of that same emotion returning again. To achieve this, simply share the story of letting go of the attachment with a trusted friend. In doing so, you will declare that you have moved beyond that attachment, and you will create accountability and support in keeping that attachment released.

Each step of the *Manifesting for Non-Gurus* approach is important, but letting go of attachments is the one which we hear the most stories about from clients. It is probably the step that is newest to most people, one which we have simply never been taught to do.

I recently experienced a vivid reminder of the power of letting go of attachments. My son Duncan, at 14, had let his hair grow long and it irritated me to no end. He is quite the athlete, and watching his hair flop around on the basketball court or the baseball field, I became more and more annoyed. In my opinion, his appearance did not match who he really is as a person.

I periodically let my frustration boil over and told him that I thought he should cut his hair, but my "shoulds" were always met with stubborn resistance. Eventually, I decided to have one last conversation with Duncan about his hair and then forget about it. I even wrote down some notes about what I wanted to say.

Several days later, while working in my office, I found those unused notes in my briefcase. I realized in that moment that I did not need to have the conversation, because the whole hair issue simply did not seem that important to me. I looked at the notes one last time and then tossed them into the recycling bin. I did not consider it at the time, but in that moment I had completely let go of my attachment to Duncan getting his hair cut.

THAT VERY SAME DAY, when I returned home from work, I entered the house and saw Duncan coming around the corner. I barely recognized him. He had taken the clippers in my bathroom and buzzed off all of his hair. After recovering from the initial shock, I asked him, "Why did you do that?" He answered, "I don't know, I just decided it was time." Clearly pleased with himself for shocking me, he turned around and went happily on his way.

Don't get me wrong here, I am NOT saying that because I let go of my attachment to Duncan getting his hair cut it actually happened. In my experience, this kind of "what's in it for me" approach absolutely does not work. What I do believe, however, is that my attachment to Duncan's hair, my <u>need</u> for him to cut it, was part of what was *preventing* him from doing it. He knew that I wanted him to cut his hair; he knew that I thought he "should" cut his hair and I believe my wanting had created resistance in him, preventing him from doing what he had probably wanted to do anyway!

Don't we all hate it when someone tells us we "have to" do something? It goes against the belief in our hearts which we all know to be true, that we do not **HAVE** to do anything. Our actions will have consequences, but part of taking 100% responsibility for our lives is knowing that we are able to make our own choices, and nobody can force us to do anything.

I believe when I truly let go of my attachment to Duncan cutting his hair, he felt it on some level. I did not cause him to cut his hair, but I believe that I stopped being a reason for him NOT to cut it. The amazing and often fun aspect of letting go of attachments is the magical feeling it can create. I felt like, by letting go of my attachment, I had persuaded Duncan to cut his own hair!

What About Fear?

One of the questions which often comes up when we look at attachments is, where does fear fit into this conversation? Isn't fear one of the things which we become attached to? Yes, it is, and the interesting thing about fear is that there always seems to be some other emotion underlying it. It is helpful to ask "What is the feeling behind that fear?"

When we are afraid, we set negative goals. We imagine what we do not want, and in many cases do an excellent job of tapping into the emotions that would accompany that scenario. Think about it: using the same process we have outlined here, we are in fact, manifesting more of exactly what we do not want!

Fear can be released or reversed in the same way as other emotions. Be aware, however, that there is often another emotion accompanying the circumstances that scare you. Also, the most powerful release will occur when you tap into the emotion behind what you **do** want instead of the one behind what you are afraid of. If you are afraid of failure for example, you can reverse that by searching for the emotion underlying your perception of success. You will end up with your attention being focused on what you want, and you will establish a stronger connection to the emotions and feelings which will attract the results we desire.

There are certainly many other times when we let ourselves become attached to ways of thinking that are unhelpful. The releasing-and-reversing strategy should work with any of them. As we enter the final step of the *Manifesting for Non-Gurus* approach, (taking inspired action), our goal is to be settled in a place of high intention and low attachment. Imagine this…knowing who we are and what we want, having clarity of intention, establishing a deep connection with the feelings and emotions we expect to experience when our intention is realized, and having no NEED for that intention to truly occur…

THIS is a powerful place from which to act.

RESOURCES

The following resources are highly recommended tools to learn more about how to let go of attachments:

The Sedona Method (Hale Dwoskin)

www.sedona.com

Hale Dwoskin's work is a simple but powerful approach to letting go of attachments. The "releasing" techniques Hale teaches are easy to learn and easy to incorporate into your daily life.

The Work (Byron Katie)

www.thework.org

Byron Katie's work is based on a series of powerful questions which you can ask yourself when you find that you have become attached to a particular emotion. This is another simple but effective strategy for letting go of attachments.

The RIM Method (Dr. Deb Sandella)

www.innermagician.com

Dr. Deb Sandella's work is especially useful for people who find themselves attached to emotions and feelings that have come from previous experiences. The RIM method is a wonderful way to discover the source of such emotions and then realize how to let them go.

Zero Limits (Dr. Joe Vitale & Dr. Ihaleakala Hew Len)

www.zerolimits.info

Joe Vitale's Zero Limits work is a simple way to "clear" yourself of the emotions and feelings you find limiting. In this work, you will also learn how your own emotions and feelings can limit those around you.

Action Without Vision = Chaos
Vision Without Action = Fantasy
— Michael Beckwith

STEP 5

Inspired Action

Taking action is the final step of the *Manifesting for Non-Gurus* approach. We all already know we should be taking action, so the question we will use for the journaling process is simple: **"What actions can I take to move toward my intention?"** We answer the question by brainstorming, (no bad answers!), and then we prioritize the list all the way down to at least one action we can take TODAY.

The most unique thing about the *Manifesting for Non-Gurus* approach is the frame of mind we will be in when we ask this question. Our awareness of who we are, clarity about our intentions, and connection to our desired feelings puts us in a different place than the person who sets a goal and then goes straight into action. Because we have let go of attachments, we have freed up a greater ability to receive intuitive answers to this question. The ideas we get from this powerful place are "inspired actions".

If we know we need to take action to get our desired results and we start receiving these ideas for inspired actions, why don't we always take action? We have already discussed some of the obstacles that show up in our look at letting go of attachments. If emotions like fear and doubt are appearing when you consider carrying out action, you should return to releasing and reversing. Beyond what we discussed in the previous chapter, there are a few other reasons in which often people cause delay in taking actions. These include:

"I DON'T KNOW WHAT TO DO."

Sometimes when we reach the step where we ask what we should do to attract our intended results, (especially when we are trying to attract something entirely new), the answer that comes up is *"I do not know."* There are a few ways to approach this response.

1. **Actually, you do know.** Some of the skills outlined here will specifically help you to tap into a better answer. Being clear about who you are means that you are the best person to answer this question, and having set your intentions, connected to the feelings and emotions which you want to be experiencing, and detached yourself from thought patterns which slow you down, you are now ready to receive your answers.

My dear friend Teresa Huggins teaches a simple and important technique anyone can use. It is called "pausing". When we pause, when we hear a response like "I don't know", often we will hear the answer come right through.

2. **Create an environment that will make it easier for you to hear your answers.** Often, we are so busy and have so many distractions present that it is difficult to come up with ideas for what actions to take. Leaving our normal environments (homes, offices, etc.) is often a great way to stimulate new ideas. Getting out into nature can be especially helpful.

3. **Ask others.** Do you have a mastermind group? A group of trusted friends and advisors? An accountability partner? Do you know someone who has already done what you want to do or something similar? These are examples of people you could share your intention with and question about what actions to take. You do not have to do everything alone!

"I DON'T KNOW WHERE TO START."

The opposite extreme, from not knowing what to do, is having so many ideas that you simply do not know where to start. This is actually a great problem to have, and there are several ways to deal with it effectively.

1. **Plan and Prioritize.** Often times, when it seems like there is too much to do, simply taking the time to plan and prioritize will make the next steps seem obvious and help you to realize that the overall task is not as overwhelming as you had previously thought. If you think you do not have enough time to plan, then this step is probably even more important than it would be at any other time!

2. **Break it down into smaller steps.** One way to quickly and easily move into action is by looking at the next small step instead of the whole project. My friend Mark McKergow, author of the book, "The Solutions Focus", teaches a great approach to looking at big goals and projects. He asks a three part question:

(1) "On a scale of 0-10, how would you rate your progress toward this goal?" Then, if your answer was a three for example, Mark would ask,

(2) "Why so high?" This forces you to look at everything that is currently going well, and focus your attention on **that** instead of on what you have not yet accomplished. The third part of Mark's question is,

(3) "What would it take to turn that into a four?" This question focuses on planning your next simple step instead of trying to reach all the way to the finish line at once. For most people, this reduces the pressure they feel and keeps them in motion.

3. **Just pick something!** We can sometimes paralyze ourselves when we try to decide on the "best" or "right" next step. At some point, it is better to just pick something and do that, rather than wait and gather more data before deciding. The data will come in the form of the feedback you will receive in response to whatever you pick.

"I DON'T HAVE TIME."

Sometimes we know exactly what we should do to move our projects forward, but think that we do not have the time necessary to make it happen. To some degree, this relates back to the idea that we just discussed about breaking projects down into smaller steps. We can all find the time to do *something* which will move our respective projects forward. In many cases, doing one small thing, and then another and another and another, suddenly carries people to a place further along than they would have thought was possible. It is like the old joke, "How do you eat an elephant?" One bite at a time...

Another way to find the time for taking actions, toward realizing your intention, is by devoting less time to the activities that do not support that intention. In each of our days, we spend time on activities that are not helping us move in the direction we want to go. The statistics reporting how many hours of television the average American watches per day, (more than four, according to the A.C. Nielsen Company), indicate it may actually be easier than we think to find a little extra time for taking action toward achieving our intentions.

Yet another way to free up some time is by asking others for help. We can delegate to others some or all of the tasks we are performing which are not the best use of our time. If you think that you cannot do that, you may want to think again. Have you considered what a local teenager can do to help you with simple tasks in your business or at home? Have you considered the fact that you might be able to barter with someone for their services? If you are looking for ways to get help, and you are willing to be creative, you will be amazed by what you find.

The Importance of Trying

"Try not! Do or do not, there is no try."
- Yoda (from the movie "Star Wars")

"Trying" has suffered a bad name. In fact, when it comes to taking action, it is important for you to be willing to try new things. There is one important distinction though: it is critical to "try" with positive expectations. If you are attempting something new with the expectation that it will not work, then I agree with Yoda: there is no point. If you are trying something new with positive expectations though, and are willing to accept and respond to feedback, then I say go for it! Once you receive that feedback, you can do more of what is working for you and less of what is not, and then you can try even more new tasks!

Trying something new is often difficult and awkward, but consider all the things you have already mastered…Remember how awkward they were when you began attempting them? Have you ever watched a child learn to walk? Or taught a teenager how to drive? Now, you can walk without thinking and drive while talking on the phone, eating a sandwich and changing the radio station! It all started with just a willingness to try something new and uncomfortable.

Another key element for staying in action towards the realization of your intentions is the willingness to say no and to make your own intention just as important as those of everyone else. Many people hate to say "no", and end up with no time and energy left for themselves. One of the biggest benefits of the *Manifesting for Non-Gurus* method is that it will make it easier for you to say no. Your clarity about who you are, what your intentions are, and what the feelings and emotions you associate with it are will empower you to be able to stand up for what is most important to you personally. Think about it as saying no to good things so that you can say yes to great ones.

"ACTING AS IF"

You may have heard the expression "acting as if" in describing a way to accelerate progress toward your goals. The idea is to think and act in the same way that a person who has already achieved what you want to achieve would. This is a powerful technique, AND it is important to make a critical distinction, especially for setting intentions in the areas of career and finance. In some cases, it can be best to think and act as successful people do *on their way to* becoming successful, instead of acting as they do once they have already achieved success. An obvious example of this would be handling money: it is better to be a good steward of your funds while you work towards success than it would be to go out and buy the Porsche which you intend to drive once your business has become a huge success.

"LIFE LONG LEARNING"

Finally, continue to learn! Information is so easily accessible to us these days, and in order to remain a leader in your field it is important to seek out and become a life-long learner. It is also imperative, however, not to let learning get in the way of taking action. Let your learning instead put you in the position to take more effective actions. If you are always learning and never doing, then you are not manifesting!

The *Manifesting for Non-Gurus* approach is not a tool for avoiding action, it is a way to ensure that the actions you are taking are inspired. Inspired actions do not feel like work: they do not seem like they require effort. When your actions are driven by clarity about who you are and what your intentions are, when you have established a strong connection to your desired feelings and emotions, and when you have let go of attachments, then your actions will become easy and effortless.

We may not like to do dishes for example, but if we do them from a place of appreciating a clean kitchen then it will not feel so much like work. We may not particularly like to run, but if we run as a way to fulfill our vision of being healthy and energetic, then we will be much more likely to enjoy it.

The next part of this step of the journaling process is also important. Select at least one action on your list and circle it, symbolizing your commitment to complete that action within the next 24 hours. It can be something small, but you should do this for at least one action every day. This relates back to the value which we already discussed of breaking our big goals down into smaller steps. Persistent and consistent action, even if the steps are small, is vital to the manifestation process.

Another valuable approach is to consider what action we could complete in the next fifteen minutes. In our seminars, we often take a fifteen minute break and give the group an assignment to execute one action that will move them in the direction of achieving their intended result. It is amazing how much can be accomplished in fifteen minutes, and it is especially exciting to see how taking one small action will make people excited about their next steps. So often, the most important step is the first one, even if it is small.

My friend, Raymond Aaron, teaches a wonderful approach to goal-setting which fits perfectly with this discussion about the value of taking small steps. Raymond teaches people to "MTO" their goals. MTO stands for Minimum, Target, and Outrageous. For any general goal, he suggests setting minimum, target and outrageous benchmarks.

An example of this could be a goal to organize your office. The minimum goal might be to file one stack of papers, (something you absolutely know you can do). The target goal might be to clear off your entire desk. Lastly, the outrageous outcome might be to hire an outside consultant who will help you completely reorganize your work space. The idea here is that by starting with the minimum goal, you get yourself into action quickly and easily and can often arrive at the target or outrageous level much faster and with far less effort.

Manifesting is not about magically creating results without taking action. It is about taking actions toward our desired results that do not feel like they are hard work or effort. It is absolutely possible to quickly and easily attract the results we want when we have the right mindset, and take inspired actions.

<u>CONCLUSION</u>

You may be extremely surprised at the results which you can achieve in a very short period of time by using the five simple steps of the *Manifesting for Non-Gurus* method. There is incredible power in knowing who you are, knowing your intentions, being connected to the feelings and emotions you desire, letting go of attachments, and consistently taking inspired action.

If you are feeling stuck, or if you become aware of being in a state of mind that is not condusive to the direction in which you wish to go, I suggest that you return to the beginning of this approach. Ask yourself, "Who am I?" Remind yourself that the negative feelings and emotions which you are experiencing are not who you have chosen to be. In reminding yourself of who you are, what you are intending to manifest, and how you will feel once you have manifested it, and then undergoing the simple process of letting go of your attachments, you can quickly move back on track. This ability to realign your thoughts when you become aware of drifting off-track is one of the most valuable benefits of understanding the *Manifesting for Non-Gurus* approach.

Imagine a community of like-minded people living their lives with clarity of purpose, intention and feeling… A community of people who act from present-moment awareness without attachments... A community of people who support each other in living the lives of their dreams… This is the community we are creating.

Now that you have completed this book, we consider you as a member of that community. Welcome!

You have reached the most important part of this book. The part where you will either put it down and say, "that was nice", or actually open up your journal and USE what you have just learned!

I cannot emphasize strongly enough the importance of taking the latter approach. Whatever benefit you receive from the insight you have gained by reading this material will be magnified many times over if you use your journal to transition what you have learned into action. With your best interests in mind, I implore you now to open up your journal and put what you have learned into ACTION!!!

Most of us have lived a life of *unconsciously attracting* the results we get. In most cases, this means we have created very few results that are in alignment with who we are and what we desire. Instead, we react to the external influences we are constantly bombarded with and respond accordingly.

Now, you are aware of how the manifestation process works, and have the opportunity to begin CHOOSING to have your manifestations be driven by mission, vision, purpose and feeling. Daily journaling is the next step in that process.

I believe that we are all capable of manifesting without an organized process like journaling. But, I also believe that most of us are not yet ready to take that step. What I have observed with our coaching clients is that the process of using this journal moves them rapidly in the direction of easily attracting their desired results. Journaling helps to make intentional manifestations a habit.

One day, we might be able to set aside the journal and live a life of clarity of purpose, clarity of intention, connection to feeling; and lack of attachment without it. That will be the day we have become master manifesters. Until then, I invite you to journal with me daily; quickly and easily attracting your desired results.

"If you are going to live a life of pure present moment awareness you had better have a personal assistant who doesn't…"

- Yakov Smirnoff

THE JOURNALING PROCESS

STEP BY STEP

The following is a step-by-step explanation of the *Manifesting for Non-Gurus* journaling process. Keep in mind that when you are using this approach, you will first be going through what we call a "process of inquiry", asking yourself questions and seeking the answers. After a while, you will then find that the process shifts to a series of reminders, rather than questions to which we are seeking answers. These reminders are equally as important as the process of inquiry. Reminding yourself of each of these steps on a consistent basis is the key to establishing new thought patterns and habits.

WHO AM I?

The first part of what we ask/remind ourselves of is who we are. We look at this question in four different ways:

1. CORE SELF – Who are you beyond your body, roles, mind and accomplishments? This is often expressed as an emotion or feeling that you would like to give and/or receive more of. This is who you truly are.

2. ROLES – Although we are not, at a core level, our roles, those roles are one of the universal ways in which we express who we really are. What are my roles?

3. SKILLS, TALENTS AND ABILITIES – This is the other way that we express who we are. These things are what we love to do and/or what we do very well. What are my skills, talents and abilities?

4. CONTRIBUTIONS – What contribution do you wish to make as you express who you truly are through your roles, skills, talents and abilities? How do you want to make the world a better place? How can you help others?

WHAT AM I INTENDING TO ATTRACT?

Now it is time to set your goal, declaring what it is you want to manifest. It is important to be sure that your intention is in alignment with who you are, otherwise you need to reassess that intention. Once you are sure your intention is in alignment with who you are, then ask yourself three important follow-up questions:

1. *Is it possible?* You do not need to be *certain* that you will attract your intention, or even that it is *likely* for that to happen. Just recognize that it is possible.

2. *Is it okay?* It is important to be free of any concerns about what other people will think.

3. *Am I ready?* Manifestation can happen very quickly...are you ready for your intention to show up NOW?

If the answer to all three of these questions is YES, then you are ready to move on and ask...

HOW WILL I FEEL?

This is the simplest of the five journaling steps. We are asking for you to imagine the emotional feelings you will experience upon achieving your intention. Repeat that intention to yourself and "flash-forward" to a time when you have already accomplished it (it is done!), considering how you will *feel* at that very moment. It can also be helpful, to imagine what you will see, hear, taste, smell and physically feel once you have achieved your intention.

Whenever possible, after writing down the words to explain it, you should close your eyes and deeply connect to that feeling of achieving your intention. This is the language of the law of attraction.

LETTING GO OF ATTACHMENTS…

Now it is time to accelerate your results by letting go of the thought patterns that slow you down. We look at letting go of attachments in four different ways:

1. APPRECIATION – List all of the things which you are appreciative of, especially in the area of your life in which you are intending to attract

your new result. Ideally, you should experience a feeling of gratitude and appreciation to such a degree that you do not really care whether you actually achieve your intention. High intention and low attachment is key!

This is the point in the journaling process where we shift from simply asking and answering questions. To use the next three steps, repeat your intention to yourself. Listen for any resistance that comes up in your mind, and then either release or turn around that resistance.

Remind yourself of:

2. INFINITE POSSIBILITIES – You do not need to know how you will attract your intention, and you do not need to do it yourself. You do not need to know exactly when the results will show up.

3. ALLOW – Allow others to have their own opinions of you. Be aware of how your actions will affect others (consideration), but do not be driven by their opinions.

4. ACCEPT – Accept, without judgment, others as they are and yourself as you are, remembering that in any given moment we are all doing the very best we can with the awareness, skills and knowledge (ASK), that are available to us.

INSPIRED ACTION...

Now that you are clear about who you are and what you are intending to attract, you are connected to the feelings and emotions associated with your intentions and you have let go of your attachments, what are the specific actions you can take to move in the direction of your intention? Brainstorm, make a list, and then choose at least one action that you can complete in the next 24 hours.

Repeat at least once daily.

Tips for Getting Maximum Benefit From Your Journal

1. Use your journal at least once every day for 30 days. There is something powerful about focusing for a full month on this new approach to accomplishing what you want. The journal has been intentionally set up to take a minimum amount of time each day, and I promise you it will be time well spent! Carry the journal with you or leave it in a conspicuous place so you are sure to remember to use it. Schedule journaling appointments in your calendar for each of the 30 days. Do whatever it takes to make this a habit.

    One of the most effective ways of learning is through repetition, and one of the most valuable aspects of the 30-day journaling process is identifying an important goal and staying focused on that goal and the feelings and necessary actions associated with it. Keeping them in your primary awareness every day will establish new thought patterns.

2. The daily journaling process can be completed
    very quickly, AND I encourage you to pause
    during the process for a few moments to
    experience the feelings and emotions that
    emerge as you complete the pages. Notice
    if they are supportive and encouraging. Are
    they the feelings and emotions you want to
    be experiencing? If they are, then experience
    them deeply and embrace them. If they are
    not, then welcome that and, to whatever
    degree you can, shift your state of mind to one
    that is more supportive. You will learn more in
    the following pages about how to accomplish
    this. If the feelings and emotions that show up,
    when you imagine that your goal has already
    been achieved are consistently NOT the kinds
    of feelings and emotions that you want to be
    experiencing, you may want to reassess your
    goal.

3. It is perfectly okay and, in fact, encouraged,
    for you to repeat the same journal entry
    on multiple days. In the beginning, your
    journaling will be a process of asking yourself
    questions and determining the answers. We

call this the "process of inquiry". Over a period of time, this process will evolve into a series of reminders. Both of these stages are very valuable.

4. Whenever possible, write in your journal first thing in the morning and at the end of the day. Ideally, you will complete full pages in both the morning and the evening. At the very least, write during one of those times and use the other as your review time. If you fill out your page in the morning, review it in the evening before you go to bed. If you fill it out in the evening, review it in the morning when you wake up.

   If you miss a day, start again the next day. It doesn't need to be more complicated than that. In fact, missing a day gives you an excellent opportunity to experience the value of the *Manifesting for Non-Gurus* approach. What do you think serves you better as you pursue a goal – beating yourself up for missing a day or just getting back on track the next day? We will talk more about this in Chapter 5.

Our Community Vision:

"What if everyone acted from a detached place of clarity about who they are, what they are intending to attract and how it would feel once they had attracted it?"

Who am I?

Core Self:

Roles:

Skills and Talents:

Contribution:

What am I intending to attract?

Is it possible?

Is it OK?

Am I ready?

How will I feel?

Let go of attachments.

Appreciation:

Infinite Possibility:

Accept and Allow:

Inspired actions to take:

APPENDIX ONE

INTENTION BRAINSTORMING

Each of the following seven pages lists an area in your life. On each page, brainstorm about the results you would like to attract. What would you like more of? What would you like less of? How would you like that area of your life to be different?

In brainstorming, there are no right or wrong answers. The idea is to simply write down everything that comes to mind. You can sort it all out later.

Ideally, give yourself at least 5-7 minutes per page to consider what you would like to experience in each area of your life. Take your time; even when it seems you have "run out of ideas"…you may be surprised what else shows up if you wait patiently for it. Keep asking, "What else? What else?" and write down whatever comes up.

Brainstorming works best when you are in a relaxed state of mind and a location without interruptions or distractions.

One way to gather even more data is by asking others. What do your most trusted friends, family and co-workers think?

HEALTH

RELATIONSHIPS

CAREER

FINANCIAL

PERSONAL

FUN/RECREATION

COMMUNITY/CONTRIBUTION

Our community of people using the Manifesting for Non-Gurus approach is growing every day. We offer free support resources through our website and we provide coaching, monthly teleseminars and live events for those who are interested. These are all ways to experience this work on a much deeper level and receive the support you need.

We invite you to become a member of our community by visiting our website at:

www.manifestingfornongurus.com

For further information about Manifesting for Non-Gurus, please contact:

HEARTSET, INC.
Manifesting for Non-Gurus
P.O. Box 232155
Leucadia, CA 92023
Email: info@manifestingfornongurus.com